THE KITCHEN LIBRARY

CHOCOLATE COOKING

D1136261

THE KITCHEN LIBRARY
CHOCOLATE COOKING

Carole Handslip

OCTOPUS BOOKS

CONTENTS

This edition published 1988 by
Octopus Books Limited
59 Grosvenor Street, London W1

© Cathay Books 1985
ISBN 0 7064 3245 2

Printed in Hong Kong

INTRODUCTION

Chocolate is without doubt the most popular flavouring for cakes, biscuits, confectionery and desserts, both for the cook and the consumer. It's simple to use, effective – and delicious.

Chocolate can be used in a multitude of ways. It can be transformed into a luscious Sachertorte, a sumptuous sticky fudge cake, a dark rich chocolate mousse or tempting truffles. It has an affinity with rum and brandy; its flavour is also enhanced by orange-flavoured liqueurs such as Grand Marnier and Cointreau, as well as Tia Maria and Crème de Menthe.

The recipes in this book – for sweets, cakes, biscuits, gâteaux, desserts, ice creams, drinks and sauces – are simple to follow and planned to produce results which will be very much appreciated by family and guests. There are also interesting ideas and advice on decorating cakes and desserts to help you achieve something that not only tastes good, but looks irresistible.

NOTES
Standard spoon measurements are used in all recipes
1 tablespoon = one 15 ml spoon
1 teaspoon = one 5 ml spoon
All spoon measures are level.

Ovens should be preheated to the specified temperature.

For all recipes, quantities are given in both metric and imperial measures. Follow either set but not a mixture of both, because they are not inter-changeable.

Eggs used in the recipes are standard size, i.e. size 3 unless otherwise stated. If large eggs are specified, use size 1.

Plain chocolate is used in the recipes unless otherwise stated.

ORIGINS OF CHOCOLATE

Chocolate and cacao powder originate from cocoa beans, which are the seeds of the fruit of the cacao tree. The tree is native to the tropical areas of Central and Southern America and chocolate in the form of a dark bitter beverage was first enjoyed by the Maya and Aztec Indians 3,000 years ago.

Cocoa beans were brought to Spain by Columbus in the 16th Century and chocolate soon gained in popularity throughout the noble houses of Europe, although the chocolate that Louis' courtiers drank was a far cry from that drunk by the Aztec and Maya Indians.

Chocolate was first available in England in the 1650s but remained an expensive luxury for the next 200 years. It was not until the beginning of the 19th Century that chocolate was produced in a solid form for eating. Since that time it has become increasingly popular, and today it is used throughout the world. The cocoa tree is now also cultivated in West Africa as well as the East and West Indies.

HOW CHOCOLATE IS MADE

The manufacture of chocolate entails a lengthy refining process. When the cocoa beans arrive at the factory, they are cleaned and then roasted in revolving drums, which develops their flavour. The cocoa beans are then broken into small pieces by passing them through special rollers. At the same time the shells are removed, leaving behind the pieces of roasted bean, called 'nibs'. These contain about 50 per cent of a fat which is known as 'cocoa butter'.

During the next stage the nibs are ground and then cooled to yield 'cocoa-mass'. To obtain the strongly flavoured cocoa powder used in cooking and drinks, a proportion of the cocoa butter is removed and the residue is ground to a powder.

To make plain chocolate, extra cocoa butter and powdered sugar are added to the cocoa-mass. For milk chocolate, milk is incorporated. The chocolate is still rough in texture at this stage; it is made smoother by high speed refiners, which pummel the ingredients together. To complete the process the molten chocolate is 'conched' by heavy rollers for up to 24 hours which heats and blends the ingredients together to give a uniform velvety texture.

TYPES OF CHOCOLATE

The quality of chocolate varies considerably. In order to be called chocolate rather than cake covering it must have a minimum of 34 per cent cocoa butter, which gives it a superior flavour and texture.

The cloudy film or 'bloom' that you sometimes see on chocolate is the result of the cocoa butter rising to the surface after exposure to varying temperatures. It does not affect the flavour and will disappear on melting.

The varieties of chocolate behave differently when heated and mixed with other ingredients. It is largely these properties, and of course flavour, which determines their use in cooking.

Plain chocolate

This has a rich, strong flavour and is the type most suited to the majority of recipes in this book. Its strong flavour gives a better result when blended with other ingredients. If you use it as a cake covering, add a little cream or vegetable oil; this makes it easier to use and prevents it setting quite so hard.

Milk chocolate

This has a milder flavour as it has full cream milk added to the cocoa butter. It is therefore not suitable to use in recipes where it is mixed with other ingredients, because the flavour tends to be lost. It can be used as a cake covering and is certainly popular with children. It is most effective piped on top of plain chocolate as a decoration for cakes and confectionery.

Chocolate-flavoured cake covering

This useful product has a certain amount of cocoa butter replaced by other vegetable oils. The oil becomes liquid on heating and this makes it much easier to melt and use. It is considerably cheaper than chocolate but the flavour is not so good.

It does not need liquid added to soften it when used as a cake covering, as it has a much softer texture than plain chocolate. It is therefore most useful for covering cakes or coating biscuits. It can also be used to make chocolate decorations.

Couveture chocolate

This special confectioners' chocolate has a high proportion of cocoa butter added which gives it a glossy appearance and brittle texture. It has a strong, fine flavour, is more expensive than other chocolates and more difficult to use. It is therefore best avoided unless you are skilled in handling chocolate.

Cocoa powder

Adding cocoa powder is the cheapest way of obtaining a strong chocolate flavour, especially for baking. It must be evenly blended into the mixture to obtain good results. It should either be sifted with other dry ingredients or blended with a little boiling water to form a smooth paste before adding to the recipe. It is rarely used for desserts – such as mousses or ice creams – where a smooth rich texture is required.

WORKING WITH CHOCOLATE

Chocolate work is not difficult but there are certain points that must be followed in order to avoid disasters:

To melt chocolate
Care must be taken when melting chocolate. If it is over-heated or if any steam or water gets into it, chocolate becomes stiff and granular and loses its gloss. There are two methods:

1. Break the chocolate into small pieces, or chop it, and place in a basin that fits snugly over a pan of hot water. Bring the water to the boil, turn off the heat and leave until the chocolate has melted; heat the water again if necessary. Do not allow any water to get into the basin.

2. You can melt chocolate in a saucepan over direct heat as long as you add a liquid to it, such as water, milk, cream or orange juice. Use a heavy-based pan and make sure the liquid covers the base. Heat extremely gently, stirring occasionally, until smooth.

If you do end up with a solid mass of chocolate it is sometimes possible to rectify it by adding a little vegetable oil and beating well. This will not be suitable for an icing or decorations where the chocolate must set hard, but could be used for desserts.

To pipe with chocolate
Pour the melted chocolate into a greaseproof paper piping bag and leave to cool slightly so that the consistency is not too thin. Secure the top of the bag carefully, then snip off the end and use to pipe words, straight or zig-zag lines, or circles on cakes or chocolate shapes. It is best to use chocolate rather than cake covering for writing as it is thicker and gives you more control.

To create a feather design, cover the top of a small or large round cake with plain or coffee glacé icing and immediately pipe a continuous circle of melted chocolate on top, keeping the rings an equal distance apart. Draw a pointed knife from the edge to the centre; dividing the icing into quarters, then draw the knife from the centre to the edge in between to create a scalloped effect.

Dipping chocolate
If using plain chocolate for dipping, add 1 tablespoon vegetable oil to 150 g (6 oz) chocolate when melting – it makes it softer and easier to use. Alternatively, use cake covering but the flavour will not be so good.

Drizzled chocolate
This is a simple but extremely effective way of decorating cakes, desserts and sweets. Cake covering is ideal for this as the chocolate should be thin in order to drizzle effectively. Place it in a greaseproof paper piping bag, snip off the end and drizzle quickly over the surface to be decorated.

CHOCOLATE DECORATIONS

Chocolate can be used to make a variety of decorations for cakes and desserts. They must be handled carefully as they are delicate – always make more than you require to allow for breakages.

Chocolate caraque
Pour a thin layer of melted chocolate on a marble slab or cold surface and spread, using a palette knife, until it begins to set and go cloudy. Leave until set. Using a sharp thin–bladed knife at a slight angle, push it across the chocolate with a slight sawing movement, scraping off a thin layer to form a long scroll.

Chocolate curls
Use a potato peeler to scrape curls directly from a block of chocolate. Make sure the chocolate is not too cold or the curls will not form properly and will break into small pieces.

Grated chocolate
Work with cool hands and cold chocolate. Grate it on a coarse grater directly onto the cake or dessert or onto greaseproof paper and then sprinkle on with a teaspoon.

Dipped nuts
Walnut halves, almonds or brazil nuts may be dipped in melted chocolate by resting the nut on a fork. Drain off as much chocolate as possible then place on greaseproof paper to set. An effective result may also be achieved by half dipping in chocolate. Strawberries can also be half dipped in this way.

Rose leaves or holly leaves

Pick fresh undamaged leaves with clearly marked veins. Wash
them and dry thoroughly. Coat the underside of each leaf with
melted chocolate using a fine paintbrush, making sure it is
spread evenly right to the edges. Allow to set chocolate side up,
then give a second coat and allow to dry. When hard, carefully
lift the tip of the leaf and peel away from the chocolate.

Squares, diamonds, triangles and circles

Spread a thin even layer of melted chocolate on a piece of
greaseproof paper. Leave until just set, but not too hard.

Cut into squares using a sharp knife and ruler. To make
triangles, cut the squares in half. To make long-sided triangles,
cut the chocolate into rectangles, then cut in half. To make
circles, cut the chocolate into small rounds using a pastry cutter.

When set, carefully lift the tip of the paper and peel away.

To store chocolate shapes

Leave to dry in a cool place, but not in the refrigerator or they
will set with a dull finish. They may be stored in an airtight
container layered with greaseproof paper for several weeks.

Bought chocolate decorations

These are satisfactory if you have no time to make your own.
if you have no time to make your own.
Chocolate vermicelli is a simple decoration for the sides of cakes.
Chocolate buttons, polka dots, flake, chocolate beanies or smarties can
be used in endless ways on the top of cakes.
Matchmakers, chocolate wafers and after dinner mints make ideal
decorations on desserts or gâteaux.

DESSERTS

CHOCOLATE AND BRANDY PUDDING

250 g (8 oz) plain
    chocolate, broken into
    pieces
4 tablespoons water
125 g (4 oz) butter
125 g (4 oz) soft brown
    sugar
1 × 439 g (15½ oz) can
    unsweetened chestnut
    purée
3 tablespoons brandy
TO FINISH:
142 ml (5 fl oz) double
    cream, whipped
chocolate caraque (see
    page 10)

Place the chocolate and water in a small pan and heat gently until melted. Leave until cool.

Place the butter, sugar and chestnut purée in an electric blender or food processor and blend until smooth. Add the chocolate and brandy and blend thoroughly. Turn into a greased 900 ml (1½ pint) charlotte mould. Leave in the refrigerator overnight.

Turn out onto a serving dish and spread some of the cream over the top. Decorate with cream whirls and chocolate caraque.
Serves 8

BLACK FOREST TRIFLE

1 Chocolate Swiss Roll (see page 66), filled with 5 tablespoons black cherry jam
3 tablespoons kirsch
1 × 425 g (15 oz) can black cherries, drained and stoned
3 egg yolks
1 tablespoon cornflour
25 g (1 oz) caster sugar
450 ml (¾ pint) milk
¼ teaspoon almond essence
142 ml (5 fl oz) double cream, whipped
fresh black cherries to decorate (optional)

Slice the Swiss roll and arrange in a glass bowl. Sprinkle with the kirsch and cherries, reserving a few if using for decoration.

Cream the egg yolks with the cornflour and sugar. Bring the milk to the boil, pour onto the egg yolks and stir well. Return to the pan and cook gently, stirring constantly, until the mixture coats the back of a wooden spoon. Add the almond essence, pour over the cherries and leave to cool.

Spread three quarters of the cream over the custard. Pipe the rest into rosettes over the top. Decorate with fresh or reserved canned cherries.
Serves 4

PEARS BELLE HÉLÈNE

900 ml (1½ pints) water
175 g (6 oz) sugar
pared rind of 1 orange
6 pears
1 quantity Chocolate
  Orange Sauce (see page
  84)
2 tablespoons chopped
  almonds, browned

Put the water, sugar and orange rind in a pan; heat gently until dissolved.

Peel the pears, leaving the stalks on, place in the syrup, cover and poach very gently for 20 to 30 minutes. Leave to cool in the syrup with the lid on.

Remove the pears with a slotted spoon. Halve, discarding the cores, and place on individual serving dishes. Spoon over the Chocolate Orange Sauce and sprinkle with the almonds.
Serves 6

CHOCOLATE LIQUEUR CRÊPES

125 g (4 oz) plain flour
1 tablespoon cocoa powder
1 tablespoon soft brown
   sugar
1 egg, beaten
300 ml (½ pint) milk
1 tablespoon oil
FILLING:
2 tablespoons cornflour
2 tablespoons caster sugar
150 ml (¼ pint) milk
2 eggs, separated
50 g (2 oz) plain
   chocolate, finely
   chopped
2 tablespoons Grand
   Marnier
grated rind of 1 orange
GLAZE:
25 g (1 oz) butter, melted
icing sugar to sprinkle
TO FINISH:
1 quantity Chocolate
   Orange Sauce (see page
   84)
shredded orange rind

Sift the flour and cocoa into a bowl and make a well in the centre. Add the sugar and egg, then gradually add half the milk, stirring constantly until a thick batter is formed. Add the oil and beat thoroughly until smooth. Add the remaining milk and leave to stand for 30 minutes.

Heat a 15 cm (6 inch) omelet pan and add a few drops of oil. Pour in 1 tablespoon of the batter and tilt the pan to coat the bottom evenly. Cook until the underside is brown, then turn over and cook for 10 seconds. Turn out onto a wire rack. Repeat with the remaining batter, stacking the cooked crêpes one on top of the other.

To make the filling, blend the cornflour and sugar with a little of the milk. Bring the remaining milk to the boil and pour onto the blended cornflour, stirring. Return to the pan and cook for 3 minutes, until thickened. Stir in the egg yolks. Add the chocolate, stirring until melted, then stir in the Grand Marnier and orange rind.

Whisk the egg whites until stiff then fold into the chocolate mixture.

Spoon a tablespoon of the mixture onto each crêpe and fold into quarters, to make a triangular shape, enclosing the filling. Place on a greased baking sheet. Brush with the melted butter and sprinkle with icing sugar.

Bake in a preheated hot oven, 200°C (400°F), Gas Mark 6, for 10 to 15 minutes.

Place on a warmed serving dish, pour over a little warm Chocolate Orange Sauce and sprinkle with orange rind. Serve the remaining sauce separately.

Serves 6 to 8

PROFITEROLES

CHOUX PASTRY:
50 g (2 oz) butter or
   margarine
150 ml (¼ pint) water
65 g (2½ oz) plain flour,
   sifted
2 eggs, beaten
FILLING:
175 ml (6 fl oz) double
   cream, whipped
1 quantity Bitter
   Chocolate Sauce (see
   page 84)

Melt the butter or margarine in a large pan, add the water and bring to the boil. Add the flour all at once and beat thoroughly until the mixture leaves the side of the pan. Cool slightly, then beat in the eggs vigorously a little at a time. Put the mixture into a piping bag fitted with a plain 1 cm (½ inch) nozzle and pipe small mounds on a dampened baking sheet.

Bake in a preheated hot oven, 220°C (425°F), Gas Mark 7, for 10 minutes, then lower the heat to 190°C (375°F), Gas Mark 5, and bake for a further 20 to 25 minutes, until golden. Make a slit in the side of each profiterole and place on a wire rack to cool.

Put the cream in a piping bag fitted with a 3 mm (⅛ inch) plain nozzle and pipe a little into each profiterole.

Pile the profiteroles into a pyramid on a serving dish and pour over the chocolate sauce just before serving.
Serves 4 to 6

CHOCOLATE MOCHA POTS

125 g (4 oz) plain
   chocolate, broken into
   pieces
150 ml (¼ pint) strong
   black coffee
450 ml (¾ pint) milk
2 eggs
2 egg yolks
2 tablespoons caster sugar
TO DECORATE:
8 tablespoons whipped
   cream
8 chocolate shapes (see
   page 11)

Place the chocolate and coffee in a pan and heat gently until melted. Add the milk and stir until blended.

Beat the eggs, egg yolks and sugar together in a basin, then pour on the chocolate milk. Mix thoroughly, then strain into 8 small ovenproof pots.

Place in a roasting pan containing 2.5 cm (1 inch) water and bake in a preheated moderate oven, 160°C (325° F), Gas Mark 3, for 45 minutes, until set. Leave to cool, then chill until required.

Decorate each with a whirl of whipped cream and a chocolate shape.
Serves 8

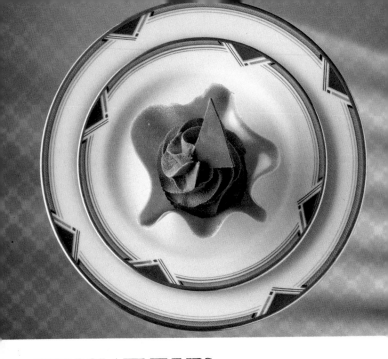

CHOCOLATE TULIPS

TULIP BASKETS:
*40 g (1½ oz) plain flour,
   sifted*
75 g (3 oz) caster sugar
3 egg whites
25 g (1 oz) butter, melted
CHOCOLATE CREAM:
*125 g (4 oz) plain
   chocolate, chopped*
*142 ml (5 fl oz) whipping
   cream*
*½ × 439 g (15 ½ oz)
   can unsweetened
   chestnut purée*
1 tablespoon caster sugar
2 tablespoons brandy
TO DECORATE:
*8 chocolate triangles (see
   page 11)*

Mix the flour and sugar in a bowl.
Add the egg whites and butter; beat
until smooth. Place 3 tablespoons of
the mixture on a non-stick baking
sheet and spread to form a 13 cm
(5 inch) round. Repeat with
remaining mixture.

Bake in a preheated moderately hot
oven, 200°C (400°F), Gas Mark 6, for
4 to 5 minutes, until the edge is golden.

Leave to cool slightly, then remove
with a plastic spatula and place each
one top side down over the base of an
inverted glass, moulding to give wavy
edges. Leave to set, then remove carefully. Repeat with remaining rounds.

Heat the chocolate and cream in a
small pan gently until melted; cool.

Blend the chestnut purée, sugar,
chocolate and brandy in a blender or
food processor until smooth.

Place the mixture in a piping bag,
fitted with a large fluted nozzle, and
pipe into the tulip cases. Decorate
each with a chocolate triangle.
Serves 8

CHOCOLATE MOUSSE

250 g (8 oz) plain
  chocolate, broken into
  pieces
5 tablespoons black coffee
142 ml (5 fl oz) whipping
  cream, lightly whipped
4 eggs
2 egg yolks
75 (3 oz) caster sugar
15 g (½ oz) gelatine,
  soaked in 3 tablespoons
  cold water

TO DECORATE:
142 ml (5 fl oz) double
  cream, whipped
6-8 chocolate rose leaves
  (see page 11)

Place the chocolate and coffee in a small pan and heat gently until melted. Leave until cool, then add to the cream and whisk until it forms soft peaks.

Whisk the eggs, egg yolks and sugar in a bowl over a pan of boiling water, until thick and mousse-like.

Place the soaked gelatine in a bowl over a pan of simmering water until dissolved, then whisk into the mousse. Stir over a bowl of iced water until thickening, then fold in the chocolate cream. Turn into a glass serving bowl and chill until set.

Decorate the edge of the mousse with piped cream whirls and chocolate rose leaves to serve.

Serves 6 to 8

CHOCOLATE SYLLABUB

125 g (4 oz) plain chocolate, broken into pieces
3 tablespoons brandy
284 ml (10 fl oz) double cream, whipped
2 egg whites
grated chocolate to decorate

Place the chocolate and brandy in a small pan and heat very gently until melted. Stir until smooth, then leave to cool.

Whisk the cream into the cooled chocolate.

Whisk the egg whites until they stand in soft peaks then carefully fold into the chocolate mixture.

Spoon into individual glasses and sprinkle with grated chocolate. Serve immediately, with Chocolate Macaroon Fingers (see page 52).
Serves 4 to 6

CHOCOLATE WHISKY CREAMS

284 ml (10 fl oz) single cream
250 g (8 oz) plain chocolate, finely chopped
3 egg yolks
3 tablespoons whisky
TO FINISH:
1 egg white
142 ml (5 fl oz) double cream, whipped
8 chocolate rose leaves (see page 11)

Place the cream in a pan and bring just to the boil. Pour into an electric blender or food processor, add the chocolate and egg yolks and blend for 30 seconds. Add the whisky and blend for 10 seconds. Pour into 8 individual glasses and chill until set.

Whisk the egg white until stiff, fold carefully into the whipped cream then pile on top of the chocolate mixture. Decorate each serving with a chocolate rose leaf.
Serves 8

CHOCOLATE RUM CUPS

175 g (6 oz) plain chocolate, melted
RUM FILLING:
2 eggs, separated
1 tablespoon rum
50 g (2 oz) plain chocolate, melted
TO DECORATE:
chocolate curls (see page 10)

Make the chocolate cases as for Colettes (see page 87), using paper cake cases instead of sweet cases.

For the filling, add the egg yolks and rum to the melted chocolate and mix well. Whisk the egg whites until fairly stiff then carefully fold into the chocolate mixture. Remove the paper from the chocolate cases and divide the rum filling between them.

Chill before serving, decorated with chocolate curls.
Makes 8

BOÎTE AU CHOCOLAT

WHISKED SPONGE:
3 eggs
125 g (4 oz) caster sugar
75 g (3 oz) plain flour,
sifted

TO FINISH:
125 g (4 oz) plain
chocolate, melted
3 tablespoons kirsch
250 g (8 oz) strawberries
2 tablespoons icing sugar
284 ml (10 fl oz) double
cream, whipped

Make the sponge mixture as for Chocolate Whisked Sponge (page 70), omitting the cocoa, and baking it in a lined and greased 20 cm (8 inch) square cake tin. Cool on a wire rack.

Use the chocolate to make squares as described on page 11, cutting it into sixteen 5 cm (2 inch) squares.

Sprinkle the kirsch over the sponge and place on a serving plate. Set aside 6 to 8 strawberries for decoration. Slice the remainder and sprinkle with the icing sugar. Mix together well but gently, then spoon on top of the sponge.

Spread some of the cream over the sides of the cake and cover with the chocolate squares, overlapping slightly. The top edge of the chocolate should come above the top of the strawberries.

Place the remaining cream in a piping bag fitted with a fluted nozzle and pipe over the fruit. Cut the reserved strawberries in half and use to decorate the gâteau.
Serves 6

CHOCOLATE ROULADE

150 g (5 oz) plain
  chocolate, broken into
  pieces
3 tablespoons water
4 eggs, separated
150 g (5 oz) caster sugar
TO FINISH:
284 ml (10 fl oz) double
  cream, whipped
sifted icing sugar
chocolate rose leaves (see
  page 11)

Place the chocolate and water in a pan and heat gently until melted.

Whisk the egg yolks with half the sugar until thick and creamy, then whisk in the warm chocolate.

Whisk the egg whites until stiff, then whisk in the remaining sugar. Fold into the chocolate mixture.

Turn into a lined and greased 20 × 30 cm (8 × 12 inch) Swiss roll tin and bake in a preheated moderate oven, 180°C (350°F), Gas Mark 4, for 25 to 30 minutes, until firm.

Leave to cool for 5 minutes, then cover with a clean damp cloth and leave in the refrigerator overnight.

Carefully remove cloth and turn the roulade onto a sheet of grease-proof paper sprinkled thickly with icing sugar. Peel off the lining paper.

Spread three quarters of the cream evenly over the roulade and roll up like a Swiss roll. Transfer to a serving dish, pipe remaining cream on the top and decorate with chocolate leaves.
Serves 8

CHOCOLATE CHIFFON PIE

75 g (3 oz) butter or
    margarine, melted
250 g (8 oz) digestive
    biscuits, crushed
25 g (1 oz) demerara
    sugar
FILLING:
250 ml (8 fl oz) milk
200 g (7 oz) plain
    chocolate, broken into
    pieces
2 eggs, separated
15 g (½ oz) gelatine,
    soaked in 3 tablespoons
    cold water
75 g (3 oz) caster sugar
142 ml (5 fl oz) double
    cream, whipped
TO FINISH:
142 ml (5 fl oz) double
    cream, whipped
chocolate triangles (see
    page 11)

Combine the butter or margarine, biscuit crumbs and demerara sugar. Press over the base and side of a deep 23 cm (9 inch) loose-bottomed flan tin. Place in the refrigerator to harden.

Meanwhile, make the filling. Place the milk and chocolate in a pan and heat gently until melted. Bring just to the boil, then pour onto the egg yolks. Return to the pan and cook, stirring, until thickened. Add the soaked gelatine and stir until dissolved. Leave until just beginning to set.

Whisk the egg whites until stiff, then gradually whisk in the caster sugar.

Whisk the chocolate mixture into the cream, then fold in the egg whites. Turn into the crumb case and smooth the surface with a palette knife. Chill until set, then remove from the tin. Decorate with piped cream and chocolate triangles.

Serves 6 to 8

CHOCOLATE ORANGE CREAM

15 g (½ oz) gelatine
grated rind and juice of
    1 orange
600 ml (1 pint) milk
3 tablespoons cornflour
2 tablespoons caster sugar
175 g (6 oz) plain
    chocolate, broken into
    pieces
142 ml (5 fl oz) double
    cream, whipped
2 tablespoons Grand
    Marnier
TO DECORATE:
6 tablespoons whipped
    cream

Soak the gelatine in the orange juice. Blend a little of the milk with the cornflour, and bring the remaining milk to the boil.

Pour the hot milk onto the blended cornflour. Mix well, then return to the pan and add the sugar. Cook, stirring, for 2 to 3 minutes, until thickened, then add the chocolate, orange rind and soaked gelatine and stir over low heat until melted. Leave to cool, stirring occasionally to prevent a skin forming.

Fold the cream into the mixture, with the Grand Marnier, then turn into a lightly greased 900 ml (1½ pint) decorative mould and chill until set. Turn out onto a plate and decorate with whipped cream.

Serves 4 to 6

CHESTNUT AND CHOCOLATE ROULADE

3 eggs, separated
125 g (4 oz) caster sugar
125 g (4 oz) plain
  chocolate, broken into
  pieces
2 tablespoons water
1 × 439 g (15½ oz) can
  unsweetened chestnut
  purée
TO FINISH:
2 tablespoons clear honey
2 tablespoons Grand
  Marnier
142 ml (5 fl oz) double
  cream
sifted icing sugar

Whisk the egg yolks with the sugar until thick and creamy.

Heat the chocolate and water gently until melted. Mix with half of the chestnut purée then gradually whisk in the egg mixture. Whisk egg whites until fairly stiff, then fold in.

Turn into a lined and greased 20 × 30 cm (8 × 12 inch) Swiss roll tin. Bake in a preheated moderate oven, 180°C (350°F), Gas Mark 4, for 25 to 30 minutes, until firm.

Leave to cool for 5 minutes, then cover with a clean damp cloth and leave in the refrigerator overnight.

Carefully remove cloth and turn the roulade onto a sheet of grease-proof paper sprinkled thickly with icing sugar. Peel off lining paper.

Whisk remaining chestnut purée with the honey and liqueur, then whisk into the cream. Spread over the roulade and roll up like a Swiss roll. Sprinkle thickly with icing sugar.
Serves 8

CHOCOLATE MERINGUE WHIRLS

2 egg whites
125 g (4 oz) caster sugar
1 tablespoon cocoa
    powder, sifted
FILLING:
142 ml (5 fl oz) double
    cream
2 tablespoons brandy
1 teaspoon clear honey
TO FINISH:
6 chocolate rose leaves (see
    page 11)

Whisk the egg whites until stiff, then whisk in the sugar, 1 tablespoon at a time, until the mixture holds its shape. Carefully fold in the cocoa.

Line 2 baking sheets with silicone paper and draw eight 7.5 cm (3 inch) and eight 5 cm (2 inch) circles on the paper.

Put the meringue in a piping bag fitted with a 1 cm (½ inch) plain nozzle and pipe onto the circles to cover completely. Bake in a preheated very cool oven, 120°C (250°F), Gas Mark ½, for 2 hours. Transfer to a wire rack to cool.

Whip the cream, brandy and honey together until it thickens and holds its shape, then spoon into a piping bag fitted with a large fluted nozzle and pipe three quarters of it onto the large circles. Cover with the small circles.

Decorate with the remaining cream and chocolate rose leaves. Serve with Bitter Chocolate Sauce (see page 84).
Makes 8

MOCHA BRANDY RING

125 g (4 oz) plain
  chocolate, broken into
  pieces
1 tablespoon instant coffee
  powder
5 tablespoons water
125 g (4 oz) self-raising
  flour
4 tablespoons corn oil
3 eggs, separated
2 tablespoons caster sugar
BRANDY SYRUP:
2 tablespoons caster sugar
4 tablespoons boiling
  water
1 tablespoon instant coffee
  powder
3 tablespoons brandy
TO FINISH:
284 ml (10 fl oz) double
  cream, whipped
grated chocolate
chocolate shapes (see page
  11)

Place the chocolate, coffee and water in a small pan and heat gently until melted. Leave until cool.

Sift the flour into a bowl, make a well in the centre and add the oil, egg yolks and chocolate mixture. Beat with an electric mixer until smooth.

Whisk the egg whites until stiff, then whisk in the sugar. Fold into the chocolate mixture and turn into a greased 23 cm (9 inch) ring mould. Bake in a preheated moderate oven, 160°C (325°F), Gas Mark 3, for 35 to 40 minutes, until the cake springs back when pressed. Cool in the tin.

To make the syrup, dissolve the sugar in the water, then stir in the coffee. Cool slightly, then stir in the brandy. Spoon over the cake while still in the tin and leave until cool.

Turn out onto a serving dish. Cover with cream and mark into swirls with a palette knife. Pipe rosettes on top and sprinkle with grated chocolate. Decorate with chocolate shapes.
Serves 6 to 8

CHOCOLATE ORANGE CHARLOTTE

200 g (7 oz) orange-
    flavoured chocolate cake
    covering, broken into
    pieces
150 ml (¼ pint) water
300 ml (½ pint) milk
15 g (½ oz) gelatine
grated rind and juice of
    1 orange
2 eggs, separated
50 g (2 oz) caster sugar
284 ml (10 fl oz)
    whipping cream,
    whipped
TO FINISH:
142 ml (5 fl oz) double
    cream, whipped
about 28 langue de chat
    biscuits
shredded orange rind to
    decorate

Place the chocolate orange cake
covering a small pan with the water.

Heat gently until melted, then stir
in the milk and bring just to the boil.
Meanwhile soak the gelatine in the
orange juice.

Beat the egg yolks, sugar and
orange rind together until creamy,
pour on the chocolate mixture and
stir well. Return to the pan and cook
gently, stirring, until the custard
thickens. Add the soaked gelatine,
stirring until dissolved. Leave to cool.

Stir over a bowl of iced water until
the mixture starts to thicken, then
fold in the whipped cream and finally
the whisked egg whites. Turn into a
lightly oiled 1.5 litre (3 pint) charlotte
mould or soufflé dish. Chill until set.

Turn out onto a plate. Cover the
side with a thin layer of cream and
press on the biscuits. Decorate with
remaining cream and orange shreds.
Serves 6 to 8

GÂTEAU DIANE

4 egg whites
250 g (8 oz) caster sugar
1 quantity chocolate
    Crème au Beurre (see
    page 81)
50 g (2 oz) flaked
    almonds, browned
25 g (1 oz) plain
    chocolate, melted

Whisk the egg whites until stiff and dry, then whisk in 2 tablespoons of the sugar. Carefully fold in the remaining sugar.

Put the meringue into a piping bag fitted with a 1 cm (½ inch) plain nozzle and pipe into three 20 cm (8 inch) rounds on baking sheets lined with silicone paper. Bake in a preheated very cool oven, 120°C (250°F), Gas Mark ½, for 2 hours. Leave to cool on the baking sheets, then peel off the lining paper.

Sandwich the meringue rounds together with one third of the crème au beurre. Spread the remaining crème around the side and on top of the meringue.

Sprinkle the almonds over the top. Put the warm chocolate in a greaseproof paper piping bag, snip off the end and drizzle the chocolate over the nuts in lines.

Serves 6

CHOCOLATE ORANGE CHEESECAKE

50 g (2 oz) butter, melted
150 g (5 oz) digestive
    biscuits, crushed
25 g (1 oz) demerara
    sugar
227 g (8 oz) cream cheese
75 g (3 oz) caster sugar
grated rind of 1 orange
2 eggs, separated
200 g (7 oz) orange
    flavoured chocolate cake
    covering, melted
142 ml (5 fl oz) double
    cream, whipped
TO DECORATE:
142 ml (5 fl oz) double
    cream, whipped
chocolate caraque (see
    page 10)

Combine the butter, biscuit crumbs and demerara sugar. Press the mixture over the base and side of a 23 cm (9 inch) loose-bottomed flan tin and place in the refrigerator to harden.

Blend the cream cheese, caster sugar, orange rind and egg yolks together, then mix in the chocolate cake covering. Fold in the whipped cream, then carefully fold in the stiffly whisked egg whites.

Turn the mixture into the crumb case and chill until set. Decorate with piped cream and chocolate caraque.

Serves 6

BRANDY WALNUT TORTE

125 g (4 oz) plain chocolate, broken into pieces
2 tablespoons water
75 g (3 oz) butter or margarine
75 g (3 oz) soft brown sugar
3 eggs, separated
2 tablespoons cornflour
125 g (4 oz) walnuts, ground
TO FINISH:
125 g (4 oz) plain chocolate, melted
3 tablespoons brandy
142 ml (5 fl oz) double cream, whipped
grated chocolate

Place the chocolate and water in a pan and heat gently until melted.

Cream the butter or margarine and sugar until light and fluffy. Beat in the egg yolks one at a time, adding the cornflour with the last two. Beat in the chocolate, then the walnuts.

Whisk the egg whites until fairly stiff, then carefully stir 1 tablespoon into the mixture to lighten it. Fold in the remainder.

Turn the mixture into a greased 500 g (1 lb) loaf tin and bake in a preheated moderate oven, 160°C (325°F), Gas Mark 3, for 1 hour 10 minutes, until the cake springs back when lightly pressed. Leave in tin for 2 minutes, then turn onto a wire rack to cool.

Use the chocolate to make fourteen 5 cm (2 inch) squares (see page 11). Prick the cake with a fork and pour over the brandy. Place on a serving plate. Spread some cream on the sides of the gâteau; pipe the remainder on top. Press the chocolate squares on to the sides and decorate the top with grated chocolate.
Serves 6 to 8

GÂTEAU GANACHE

4 egg whites
250 g (8 oz) caster sugar
few drops of vanilla
    essence
1 teaspoon vinegar
125 g (4 oz) hazelnuts,
    ground and toasted
FILLING:
175 g (6 oz) plain
    chocolate, broken into
    pieces
150 ml (¼ pint) water
50 g (2 oz) caster sugar
250 ml (8 fl oz) double
    cream

TO FINISH:
sifted icing sugar
8 chocolate shapes (see
    page 11)

Whisk the egg whites until stiff, then gradually whisk in the sugar. Continue whisking until the meringue is very stiff. Carefully fold in the vanilla, vinegar and hazelnuts.

Divide the mixture between two lined and greased 20 cm (8 inch) sandwich tins and spread evenly. Bake in a preheated moderate oven, 180°C (350°F), Gas Mark 4, for 45 to 50 minutes. Cool on a wire rack.

Heat the chocolate, water and sugar in a pan gently until dissolved, then boil for 10 minutes; cool.

Add 4 tablespoons of the chocolate sauce to the cream, then whip until it stands in soft peaks. Sandwich the meringue rounds together with three quarters of the cream and dust the top with icing sugar. Pipe the remaining cream around the edge and decorate with the chocolate shapes. Serve with the remaining chocolate sauce.

Serves 6

ICES AND BOMBES

CHOCOLATE MINT ICE

MINT ICE CREAM:
3 egg yolks
150 g (5 oz) caster sugar
284 ml (10 fl oz) single
  cream
284 ml (10 fl oz) double
  cream, whipped
3 tablespoons crème de
  menthe
few drops of green food
  colouring
TO SERVE:
25 g (1 oz) plain
  chocolate, melted
1 quantity Bitter
  Chocolate Sauce (see
  page 84)

Make the ice cream as for Chocolate Chip Ice Cream (page 38), replacing the chocolate drops and vanilla with the crème de menthe and colouring.

Turn into a 1 kg (2 lb) loaf tin, cover with foil, seal and freeze until firm.

Dip tin into cold water to loosen the ice cream and turn out onto a chilled dish. Place in the refrigerator for about 15 minutes to soften.

Place the warm chocolate in a greaseproof paper piping bag and snip off the end. Cut the ice cream into slices and place on serving plates. Drizzle the chocolate across each slice and serve with the chocolate sauce.
Serves 6

CHOCOLATE BRANDY BOMBES

175 g (6 oz) plain
   chocolate, broken into
   pieces
3 tablespoons water
2 eggs, separated
125 g (4 oz) caster sugar
284 ml (10 fl oz) double
   cream
2 tablespoons brandy
75 g (3 oz) meringues,
   broken into pieces

TO SERVE:
1 quantity Bitter
   Chocolate Sauce (see
   page 84)

Place the chocolate and water in a small pan and heat gently until melted. Stir in the egg yolks and leave to cool.

Whisk the egg whites until they form stiff peaks, then gradually whisk in the sugar.

Whip the cream and brandy together until soft peaks form, then fold in the chocolate mixture. Carefully fold in the whisked egg whites and broken meringues.

Turn into a 1.5 litre (2½ pint) pudding basin, or into eight 175 ml (6 fl oz) individual moulds, cover with foil, seal and freeze until firm.

Dip each mould into warm water and turn out onto a serving dish. Pour some of the chocolate sauce over the top and serve the rest separately.
Serves 8

FESTIVE ICES

125 g (4 oz) glacé
  cherries, quartered
25 g (1 oz) angelica,
  chopped
50 g (2 oz) crystallized
  pineapple, chopped
125 g (4 oz) raisins
3 tablespoons rum
3 egg yolks
75 g (3 oz) caster sugar
284 ml (10 fl oz) single
  cream
284 ml (10 fl oz) double
  cream, whipped
CHOCOLATE RUM SAUCE:
90 ml (3 fl oz) single
  cream
125 g (4 oz) plain
  chocolate, broken
  into pieces
2 tablespoons rum
TO DECORATE:
chocolate holly leaves (see
  page 11)

Place the fruits in a bowl, pour over
the rum and leave to soak for 1 hour.

Beat the egg yolks and sugar
together until creamy.

Bring the single cream just to the
boil. Pour immediately onto the egg
mixture, stirring vigorously. Pour
into a heatproof bowl over a pan of
hot water and heat gently until
thickened. Strain and leave to cool.

Fold the whipped cream into the
cooled custard. Pour into a rigid
freezerproof container, cover, seal
and freeze for about 2 hours. Whisk
well, then fold in the fruit and rum.
Divide between six 175 ml (6 fl oz)
individual moulds, cover with foil
and freeze until firm.

To make the sauce, put the cream,
chocolate and rum in a pan and heat
gently, stirring until smooth; cool.

Dip the moulds into cold water and
turn out onto chilled serving plates.
Pour the sauce around the ices and
serve immediately, decorated with
chocolate leaves.
Serves 6

PRALINE BOMBITAS

PRALINE ICE CREAM:
3 egg yolks
150 g (5 oz) caster sugar
2 tablespoons instant
  coffee powder
284 ml (10 fl oz) single
  cream
284 ml (10 fl oz) double
  cream
125 g (4 oz) praline,
  ground (see page 88)
TO FINISH:
175 g (6 oz) plain
  chocolate cake covering,
  melted and cooled
1 quantity Fudge Sauce
  (see page 82)

Make the ice cream as for Chocolate
Chip Ice Cream (page 38), dissolving
the coffee powder in the single cream
during heating and replacing the
chocolate chips with the praline. Turn
into a rigid freezerproof container,
cover, seal and freeze until firm.

Scoop out small balls onto a foil-
lined baking sheet and open-freeze for
about 4 hours, until hard.

Support each ice cream ball on the
rounded end of a skewer and dip
quickly into the melted chocolate.
Shake off any excess chocolate and
return to the baking sheet. Open-
freeze for 30 minutes. Serve
immediately, with the sauce.
Serves 4 to 6

CHOCOLATE CHIP ICE CREAM

3 egg yolks
125 g (4 oz) caster sugar
284 ml (10 fl oz) single cream
284 ml (10 fl oz) double cream, whipped
½ teaspoon vanilla essence
100 g (3 ½ oz) plain chocolate drops

Beat the egg yolks and sugar together until creamy. Bring the single cream to the boil, pour onto the egg yolks and mix thoroughly. Transfer to the top of a double boiler, or a heatproof bowl over a pan of hot water, and cook, stirring constantly, until thick enough to coat the back of the spoon. Strain into a bowl and leave until cool.

Fold into the whipped cream with the vanilla essence, then pour into a rigid freezerproof container, cover, seal and freeze for about 2 hours.

Remove from the freezer and whisk well, then fold in the chocolate drops. Return to the freezer until firm.

Transfer to the refrigerator about 45 minutes before serving to soften. Scoop into chilled glasses to serve.
Serves 6 to 8

DARK CHOCOLATE ICE CREAM

2 eggs
2 egg yolks
75 g (3 oz) caster sugar
284 ml (10 fl oz) single
　cream
200 g (7 oz) plain
　chocolate, broken into
　pieces
284 ml (10 fl oz) double
　cream, whipped
TO SERVE:
chocolate curls (see page
　10)

Mix the eggs, egg yolks and sugar together. Place the single cream and chocolate in a pan and heat gently until melted, then bring to the boil. Pour onto the egg mixture, stirring vigorously, then transfer to the top of a double boiler, or to a heatproof bowl over a pan of boiling water, and cook, stirring constantly, until thick enough to coat the back of the spoon. Strain into a bowl and leave to cool.

Fold into the whipped cream, then pour into a rigid freezerproof container. Cover, seal and freeze for about 2 hours. Remove from the freezer, whisk well, then refreeze until firm.

Transfer to the refrigerator 45 minutes before serving to soften. Scoop into chilled glasses and serve immediately, sprinkled with chocolate curls.
Serves 8

FROZEN CHOCOLATE SOUFFLÉ

*125 g (4 oz) plain
   chocolate, broken into
   pieces
3 tablespoons water
4 eggs, separated
125 g (4 oz) caster sugar
284 ml (10 fl oz) double
   cream, whipped*
TO SERVE:
*50 g (2 oz) chocolate
   caraque (see page 10)*

Tie a double band of foil around a
900 ml (1½ pint) soufflé dish to stand
5 cm (2 inches) above the rim.

Place the chocolate and water in a
small pan and heat gently until
melted. Leave to cool slightly.

Put the egg yolks and sugar in a
bowl and whisk with an electric
beater until thick and mousse-like.
Whisk in the chocolate, then carefully
fold in the cream.

Whisk the egg whites until stiff and
fold 1 tablespoon into the chocolate
mixture to lighten it. Carefully fold
in the remaining egg white, then pour
into the prepared soufflé dish and
level the surface. Open-freeze
overnight until firm.

Remove the foil band carefully and
place the soufflé in the refrigerator
20 minutes before serving to soften.
Cover the top with the chocolate
caraque.
Serves 8

COFFEE CABANAS

CHOCOLATE CAKE:
75 g (3 oz) plain
    chocolate, broken into
    pieces
50 g (2 oz) butter or
    margarine
125 g (4 oz) caster sugar
50 g (2 oz) self-raising
    flour, sifted
2 eggs

COFFEE ICE CREAM:
2 tablespoons instant
    coffee powder
2 tablespoons boiling
    water
2 egg whites
125 g (4 oz) caster sugar
284 ml (10 fl oz) double
    cream
50 g (2 oz) walnuts,
    chopped

TO SERVE:
Bitter Chocolate Sauce
    (see page 84)

Make and bake the chocolate cake as for Pecan Brownies (page 56), omitting the pecan nuts. Cool in the tin, then turn out and split in half horizontally.

To make the ice cream, mix the coffee and water together and leave to cool. Whisk the egg whites until stiff, then gradually whisk in the sugar. Whip the cream with the coffee until it forms soft peaks, then fold in the meringue mixture and walnuts.

Place the bottom half of the cake in the cleaned cake tin. Spoon the ice cream over the top and spread evenly to the edges. Top with the remaining cake and press together firmly. Cover with foil, seal and freeze overnight.

Dip the tin in warm water to loosen the cake and turn out onto a chilled serving plate. Cut in half lengthwise, then into slices. Serve with the chocolate sauce.
Serves 8

BOMBE AU CHOCOLAT

1 quantity Dark
    Chocolate Ice Cream
    (see page 39)
142 ml (5 fl oz) double
    cream
1 tablespoon kirsch
1 tablespoon icing sugar,
    sifted
50 g (2 oz) ratafias,
    halved

Leave the ice cream at room
temperature for 30 minutes to soften.
Chill a 1.5 litre (2½ pint) bombe
mould or pudding basin in the
refrigerator.

Whip the cream, kirsch and icing
sugar together until stiff peaks form,
then fold in the ratafias.

Line the mould or basin thickly
with the chocolate ice cream. Fill the
centre with the cream and cover with
any remaining ice cream. Put on the
lid of the bombe mould or cover the
basin with foil, seal and freeze
overnight.

Dip the mould or basin into cold
water to loosen the bombe and turn
out onto a chilled serving plate to
serve.
Serves 6 to 8

VANILLA AND CHOCOLATE RING

CHOCOLATE ICE CREAM :
1 egg
1 egg yolk
40 g (1½ oz) caster sugar
142 ml (5 fl oz) single
    cream
75 g (3 oz) plain
    chocolate, broken into
    pieces
142 ml (5 fl oz) double
    cream, whipped
VANILLA ICE CREAM:
1 egg white
50 g (2 oz) caster sugar
450 ml (¾ pint) double
    cream, whipped
1 teaspoon vanilla essence
TO FINISH:
142 ml (5 fl oz) double
    cream, whipped
10-12 chocolate triangles
    (see page 11)

Make the chocolate ice cream as for
Dark Chocolate Ice Cream (page 39).
Turn into a 1.25 litre (2½ pint) ring
mould. Cover with foil and freeze for
3 hours.

To make the vanilla ice cream,
whisk the egg white until stiff, then
whisk in the sugar. Fold into the
whipped cream with the vanilla
essence. Spoon on top of the
chocolate ice cream, cover with foil,
seal and freeze overnight.

Dip the mould in warm water and
turn out the ice cream onto a chilled
serving plate. Decorate the top with
piped cream rosettes and chocolate
triangles.
Serves 8

ICED HAZELNUT GÂTEAU

75 g (3 oz) hazelnuts
75 g (3 oz) caster sugar
50 g (2 oz) plain
 chocolate, chopped
2 tablespoons water
250 ml (8 fl oz) double
 cream, whipped
2 tablespoons black coffee
3 tablespoons brandy
16 sponge fingers
TO FINISH:
142 ml (5 fl oz) double
 cream, whipped
25 g (1 oz) plain
 chocolate, melted

Put the hazelnuts and sugar in a heavy-based pan and heat gently until the sugar has melted. Cook slowly until the sugar has caramelized and the nuts are brown, tilting the pan occasionally. Turn onto an oiled baking sheet, leave until hard, then grind to a powder using a coffee grinder or food processor.

Place the chocolate and water in a small pan and heat gently until melted. Cool, then whisk into the cream. Fold in the hazelnut powder.

Mix the coffee and brandy together and quickly dip in the sponge fingers. Arrange half in a lined and greased 500 g (1 lb) loaf tin. Spread the chocolate cream on top and cover with the remaining sponge fingers. Cover with foil, seal and freeze until firm.

Dip the tin in cold water to loosen the gâteau and turn out onto a chilled serving plate. Cover with the cream.

Drizzle the cooled chocolate on top of the gâteau (see page 8). Leave in the refrigerator for 30 minutes before serving, to soften.
Serves 6

CHOCOLATE TORTONI

175 g (6 oz) plain
  chocolate, broken into
  pieces
142 ml (5 fl oz) single
  cream
2 tablespoons kirsch
284 ml (10 fl oz) double
  cream, whipped
50 g (2 oz) ratafias,
  finely crushed
TO FINISH:
40 g (1½ oz) ratafias
4 tablespoons double
  cream, whipped
8 chocolate circles (see
  page 11)

Place the chocolate and single cream in a small pan and heat gently until melted. Stir well until smooth, then leave until cool.

Whisk the kirsch and chocolate mixture into the whipped cream, then fold in the crushed ratafias. Spoon into a 500 g (1 lb) loaf tin and smooth the surface. Cover with foil, seal and freeze overnight.

Turn upside down over a chilled serving plate and rub the tin with a cloth wrung out in very hot water until the ice cream drops out.

Press the ratafia crumbs over the top and sides of the ice cream. Pipe the cream down the centre and decorate with the chocolate circles.
Serves 8

CHOCOLATE ICE BOX CAKE

WHISKED SPONGE:

2 eggs

75 g (3 oz) caster sugar

50 g (2 oz) plain flour, sifted

1 tablespoon instant coffee powder, sifted

FILLING:

250 g (8 oz) plain chocolate, broken into pieces

3 tablespoons black coffee

2 eggs, separated

2 tablespoons rum

125 g (4 oz) caster sugar

142 ml (5 fl oz) double cream, whipped

TO FINISH:

120 ml (4 fl oz) double cream, whipped

25 (1 oz) plain chocolate, melted

To make the whisked sponge, place the eggs and sugar in a heatproof bowl over a pan of hot water and whisk until thick and mousse-like. (The hot water is unnecessary if using an electric beater.) Sift the flour and coffee powder together and carefully fold into the whisked mixture. Turn into a lined and greased 20 cm (8 inch) cake tin and bake in a preheated moderately hot oven, 190°C (375°F), Gas Mark 5, for 25 to 30 minutes, until the cake springs back when lightly pressed. Cool on a wire rack.

To make the filling, place the chocolate and coffee in a small pan and heat gently until melted. Stir in the egg yolks and rum and leave to cool.

Whisk the egg whites until they form stiff peaks, then gradually whisk in the sugar.

Whisk the chocolate mixture into the cream, then carefully fold in the whisked egg whites.

Split the cake in half horizontally and place the bottom half in the cleaned cake tin. Spoon the filling over the top, spreading evenly to the edge. Cover with the remaining sponge, pressing gently together. Cover with foil, seal and freeze overnight.

Dip the tin in warm water to loosen the cake and turn out onto a chilled serving plate. Spread about half of the cream over the top of the cake. Put the cooled chocolate into a greaseproof paper piping bag, snip off the end and drizzle the chocolate across the top of the gâteau. Pipe the remaining cream around the edge.

Serves 8

SMALL CAKES AND BISCUITS

VIENNESE STARS

125 g (4 oz) butter or margarine
50 g (2 oz) icing sugar, sifted
125 g (4 oz) plain flour
25 g (1 oz) cornflour
3 tablespoons chocolate hazelnut spread
75 g (3 oz) plain chocolate, melted

Cream the butter or margarine and icing sugar together until light and fluffy. Sift in the flour and cornflour and beat until smooth. Place the mixture in a piping bag fitted with a 2.5 cm (1 inch) fluted nozzle and pipe into 3.5 cm (1½ inch) rosettes well apart on a baking sheet.

Bake in a preheated moderately hot oven, 190°C (375°F), Gas Mark 5, for 10 to 15 minutes, until pale golden. Transfer to a wire rack to cool.

Sandwich the stars together in pairs with the hazelnut spread. Dip half of each star into the chocolate and place on greaseproof paper until set.
Makes about 8

MINT CHOCOLATE ÉCLAIRS

CHOUX PASTRY:
50 g (2 oz) butter or
    margarine
150 ml (¼ pint) water
65 g (2½ oz) plain flour,
    sifted
2 eggs, beaten
142 ml (5 fl oz) double
    cream, whipped
ICING:
125 g (4 oz) plain
    chocolate, broken into
    pieces
2 tablespoons single cream
few drops of peppermint
    essence

Make the choux pastry as for
Profiteroles (page 16). Spoon into a
piping bag fitted with a 1 cm (½ inch)
plain nozzle and pipe into 7.5 cm
(3 inch) lengths on a dampened baking
sheet. Bake in a preheated moderately
hot oven, 200°C (400°F), Gas Mark 6,
for 25 minutes, until crisp and golden
brown. Make a slit in the side of each
éclair and cool on a wire rack.

Fill a piping bag fitted with a 5 mm
(¼ inch) plain nozzle with the whipped
cream and pipe into each éclair.

Melt the chocolate and single
cream in a small heatproof bowl over
a pan of hot water, add peppermint
essence to taste and mix well. Dip
each éclair into the chocolate and
place on a wire rack to set.
Makes 18 to 20

CRUNCHY CLUSTERS

125 g (4 oz) plain
  chocolate, broken into
  pieces
1 tablespoon clear honey
2 tablespoons black coffee
250 g (8 oz) granola or
  crunchy breakfast cereal
25 g (1 oz) walnuts,
  chopped

Place the chocolate, honey and coffee in a pan and heat gently until melted. Stir in the cereal and walnuts until thoroughly mixed. Spoon into paper cake cases and leave to set.
Makes 12

CHOCOLATE ROCKS

2 egg whites
125 g (4 oz) caster sugar
2 tablespoons cocoa
  powder, sifted
75 g (3 oz) almonds,
  chopped and browned
TO FINISH:
50 g (2 oz) plain
  chocolate, chopped
2 teaspoons milk

Whisk the egg whites until very stiff and dry looking. Gradually whisk in the sugar, then fold in the cocoa and all but 1 tablespoon of the almonds.

Place small mounds of the mixture on a baking sheet lined with non-stick paper and bake in a preheated moderate oven, 180°C (350°F), Gas Mark 4, for 15 to 20 minutes. Leave to cool, then remove from the paper.

Place the chocolate and milk in a small pan and heat gently until melted. Spoon a little over each 'rock' and sprinkle with the remaining nuts.
Makes about 15

CHOCOLATE MERINGUES

125 g (4 oz) caster sugar
2 tablespoons cocoa
  powder
2 egg whites
120 ml (4 fl oz) double
  cream, whipped

Sift the sugar and cocoa together.

Whisk the egg whites until stiff and dry, then whisk in the sugar mixture 1 tablespoon at a time until the mixture holds its shape. Spoon into a piping bag fitted with a 1 cm (½ inch) plain nozzle and pipe into mounds on a baking sheet lined with non-stick paper.

Bake in a preheated cool oven, 120°C (250°F), Gas Mark ½, for about 2 hours, until crisp. Leave to cool slightly, then carefully transfer to a wire rack to cool completely.

Sandwich the meringues together with the cream to serve.
Makes 6

CHOCOLATE MACAROON FINGERS

175 g (6 oz) caster sugar
150 g (5 oz) ground
    almonds
2 tablespoons ground rice
2 egg whites
½ teaspoon almond
    essence
75 g (3 oz) plain
    chocolate, melted

Mix the sugar, almonds and ground rice together and set aside. Beat the egg whites lightly, add the dry ingredients and almond essence and beat to a smooth, firm consistency.

Leave the mixture to stand for 5 minutes, then place in a piping bag fitted with a 2 cm (¾ inch) plain nozzle. Pipe into 7.5 cm (3 inch) lengths on baking sheets lined with baking parchment and bake in a preheated moderate oven, 180°C (350°F), Gas Mark 4, for 15 minutes.

Cool the macaroons on the baking sheets, then remove with a palette knife.

Dip each end of the macaroons into the melted chocolate, then place on a piece of greaseproof paper and leave until set before serving.

Makes 18 to 20

CHOCOLATE BOXES

*3-egg Chocolate Whisked
 Sponge mixture (see
 page 70)*
*175 g (6 oz) plain
 chocolate, melted*
*½ quantity vanilla Crème
 au Beurre (see page 81)
 or Butter Icing (see
 page 82)*

Turn the sponge mixture into a lined
and greased 20 cm (8 inch) square cake
tin. Bake in a preheated moderately
hot oven, 190°C (375°F), Gas Mark 5,
for 35 to 40 minutes, until the cake
springs back when lightly pressed.
Turn onto a wire rack to cool.

Use the melted chocolate to make
sixty-eight 5 cm (2 inch) squares as
described on page 11.

Split the cake in half horizontally
and sandwich together with a quarter
of the icing. Cut into 16 squares and
spread more icing round the sides.
Press a chocolate square onto each
side to form a box.

Place the remaining icing in a
piping bag fitted with a fluted nozzle
and pipe rosettes on top of each box.
Cut remaining chocolate squares into
triangles and place one on each cake.
Makes 16

CHOCOLATE FLAPJACKS

125 g (4 oz) butter or margarine
75 g (3 oz) soft brown sugar
75 g (3 oz) golden syrup
250 g (8 oz) rolled oats
125 g (4 oz) plain chocolate, melted

Place the butter or margarine, sugar and syrup in a pan and heat gently until melted. Stir in the oats and mix thoroughly. Turn into a greased shallow 20 cm (8 inch) square tin and smooth the top with a palette knife.

Bake in a preheated moderate oven, 180°C (350°F), Gas Mark 4, for 25 to 30 minutes, until golden brown.

Cool in the tin for 2 minutes, then mark into fingers. Leave until cold, then remove from the tin. Spoon the chocolate over each finger and leave until set.

Makes 16

CHOCOLATE DROPS

50 g (2 oz) plain flour
25 g (1 oz) cocoa powder
3 eggs
125 g (4 oz) caster sugar
125 g (4 oz) orange
    Butter Icing (see page
    82)

Sift the flour and cocoa together.
Place the eggs and caster sugar in a
heatproof bowl over a pan of boiling
water and whisk until thick and
mousse-like. (The hot water is
unnecessary if using an electric
beater.)

Fold in the flour mixture, then
spoon into a piping bag fitted with a
1 cm (½ inch) plain nozzle and pipe
5 cm (2 inch) rounds on greased and
floured baking sheets. Bake in a
preheated moderately hot oven,
190°C (375°F), Gas Mark 5, for
12 minutes. Cool on a wire rack.

Place the butter icing in a piping
bag fitted with a fluted nozzle and
pipe over half of the rounds.
Sandwich the plain sponge rounds
together with the iced ones.
Makes 12 to 14

CHOCOLATE PALMIERS

1 × 212 g (7½ oz)
    packet frozen puff
    pastry, thawed
75 g (3 oz) sugar
25 g (1 oz) plain
    chocolate, grated

Roll out the pastry on a surface
sprinkled with half the sugar.
Sprinkle the remaining sugar on top
of the pastry as you roll it out to a
rectangle about 30 × 25 cm (12 × 10
inches); trim the edges. Sprinkle with
the chocolate.

Take one shorter edge of the pastry
and carefully roll it up to the centre.
Roll up the other side to meet it.
Moisten the rolls with water where
they meet and press together to join.
Cut into 1 cm (½ inch) slices and
place well apart on a baking sheet,
flattening slightly with the heel of
your hand.

Bake in a preheated hot oven,
220°C (425°F), Gas Mark 7, for 10 to
12 minutes; turn them over when
they begin to brown so that both
sides caramelize. Transfer to a wire
rack to cool.
Makes 18 to 20

CHOCOLATE SHORTIES

125 g (4 oz) butter or margarine
50 g (2 oz) soft brown sugar
125 g (4 oz) self-raising flour
2 tablespoons cocoa powder
15 g (½ oz) hazelnuts, chopped

Beat the butter or margarine and sugar together until light and fluffy. Sift in the flour and cocoa and mix well. Using dampened hands, form into balls the size of a walnut and place on baking sheets. Flatten with a dampened fork and sprinkle with the hazelnuts.

Bake in a preheated moderately hot oven, 190°C (375°F), Gas Mark 5, for 10 to 15 minutes. Leave on the baking sheets for 1 minute, then transfer to a wire rack to cool.
Makes 18 to 20

CHOCOLATE CHEWS

2 egg whites
75 g (3 oz) caster sugar
150 g (5 oz) desiccated coconut
2 tablespoons cocoa powder, sifted

Whisk the egg whites until stiff, then whisk in the sugar. Carefully fold in the coconut and cocoa. Place small mounds of the mixture on a baking sheet lined with non-stick paper.

Bake in a preheated moderate oven, 180°C (350°F), Gas Mark 4, for 15 to 20 minutes, until lightly browned; the mixture will still feel soft but will crisp as it cools. Carefully remove from the paper with a palette knife when cool.
Makes 12

PECAN BROWNIES

50 g (2 oz) plain chocolate, chopped
50 g (2 oz) butter or margarine
125 g (4 oz) soft brown sugar
50 g (2 oz) self-raising flour
50 g (2 oz) pecan nuts, chopped
2 eggs, beaten

Place the chocolate, butter or margarine and sugar in a small pan and heat gently until melted.

Sift the flour into a mixing bowl, add the nuts, then beat in the eggs and chocolate mixture until smooth.

Pour into a lined and greased shallow 18 cm (7 inch) square tin. Bake in a preheated moderate oven, 180°C (350°F), Gas Mark 4, for 35 to 40 minutes, until just beginning to shrink from the sides of the tin. Leave to cool in the tin, then cut into squares.
Makes 9

FLORENTINES

75 g (3 oz) butter
75 g (3 oz) golden syrup
*25 g (1 oz) plain flour,
    sifted*
*75 g (3 oz) flaked
    almonds, coarsely
    chopped*
*25 g (1 oz) chopped
    mixed peel*
*50 g (2 oz) glacé cherries,
    coarsely chopped*
*15 g (½ oz) angelica,
    coarsely chopped .*
*125 g (4 oz) plain
    chocolate, melted*

Place the butter and syrup in a small
pan and heat gently until melted. Stir
in the flour, almonds, mixed peel,
cherries and angelica.

Place teaspoonfuls of the mixture
well apart on baking sheets lined with
non-stick paper. Flatten with a
dampened fork into 8 cm (3½ inch)
rounds. Bake in a preheated moderate
oven, 180°C (350°F), Gas Mark 4, for
8 to 10 minutes.

Leave to cool for 1 minute then,
using a plain cutter slightly larger
than the florentines, carefully place it
over each florentine and move around
to neaten the edges. Transfer to a
wire rack to cool.

Spread the chocolate over the flat
underside of each florentine. Place the
biscuits chocolate side up on a wire
rack and mark the chocolate into lines
with a fork. Leave until set.
Makes 14

CARAMEL TRIANGLES

125 g (4 oz) butter
50 g (2 oz) caster sugar
175 g (6 oz) wholemeal flour

FILLING:
125 g (4 oz) butter or margarine
50 g (2 oz) soft brown sugar
150 ml (5 fl oz) condensed milk

CHOCOLATE TOPPING:
125 g (4 oz) plain chocolate, broken into pieces
2 tablespoons milk

Cream the butter and sugar together until light and fluffy. Add the flour and stir until the mixture binds together. Knead until smooth.

Roll out to a square and press evenly into a shallow 23 cm (9 inch) square cake tin and prick well. Bake in a preheated moderate oven, 180°C (350°F), Gas Mark 4, for 25 to 30 minutes. Cool in the tin.

Place the filling ingredients in a pan and heat gently, stirring, until dissolved. Bring slowly to the boil, then cook, stirring constantly, for 5 to 7 minutes. Cool slightly, then spread over the biscuit mixture and leave to set.

For the topping, place the chocolate and milk in a pan and heat gently until melted. Spread over the caramel. Leave until set, then cut into triangles.
Makes 16

CHOCOLATE CHIP BISCUITS

125 g (4 oz) butter or
  margarine
50 g (2 oz) soft brown
  sugar
1 egg, beaten
150 g (5 oz) self-raising
  flour
175 g (6 oz) plain
  chocolate, finely
  chopped

Cream the butter or margarine and sugar together until light and fluffy. Beat in the egg, then sift in the flour. Mix in the chocolate.

Put teaspoonfuls of the mixture slightly apart on a greased baking sheet and bake in a preheated moderate oven, 180°C (350°F), Gas Mark 4, for 15 to 20 minutes, until golden brown. Transfer to a wire rack to cool.

Makes 16 to 20

CHOCOLATE CRUNCHIES

175 g (6 oz) rolled oats
50 g (2 oz) soft brown
  sugar
120 ml (4 fl oz) corn oil
1 egg
125 g (4 oz) plain
  chocolate, melted

Place the oats, sugar, oil and egg in a bowl and beat together thoroughly. Place teaspoonfuls of the mixture well apart on a greased baking sheet and flatten with a dampened fork.

Bake in a preheated moderate oven, 160°C (325°F), Gas Mark 3, for 15 to 20 minutes, until golden brown. Leave to cool for 1 minute, then transfer to a wire rack to cool completely.

Spread the chocolate over the flat underside of each biscuit. Place chocolate side up on a wire rack, leave to set slightly, then mark the chocolate into lines with a palette knife. Leave until set.

Makes 20

BRAN CRUNCH

50 g (2 oz) butter or
  margarine
2 tablespoons clear honey
125 g (4 oz) plain
  chocolate, broken into
  pieces
75 g (3 oz) bran flakes
25 g (1 oz) walnuts,
  chopped

Place the butter or margarine, honey and chocolate in a pan and heat gently, stirring, until melted. Add the bran flakes and walnuts and mix thoroughly.

Turn into a lined and greased shallow 18 cm (7 inch) square cake tin, smooth the surface and chill until set. Cut into triangles to serve.

Makes 8

NUTTY CIRCLES

50 g (2 oz) butter or
    margarine
25 g (1 oz) soft brown
    sugar
75 g (3 oz) plain flour,
    sifted
50 g (2 oz) hazelnuts,
    ground and browned
3 tablespoons chocolate
    hazelnut spread
icing sugar to sprinkle

Beat the butter or margarine and sugar together until light and fluffy. Add the flour and ground hazelnuts and stir until the mixture binds together.

Turn onto a floured surface and knead until smooth. Roll out thinly and cut into rounds using a 6 cm (2½ inch) fluted cutter. Using a 2.5 cm (1 inch) plain cutter remove the centre from 10 rounds. Gather the trimmings and discarded centres, roll out and use to cut more rounds and circles. Place the rounds and circles on baking sheets and bake in a preheated moderate oven, 160°C (325°F), Gas Mark 3, for 20 minutes, until golden. Leave to cool on the baking sheets.

Spread the plain rounds with the chocolate hazelnut spread. Sprinkle the circles with icing sugar and place on top.
Makes about 10

CHOC-NUT CURLS

75 g (3 oz) butter or
    margarine
75 g (3 oz) caster sugar
40 g (1½ oz) plain flour,
    sifted
15 g (½ oz) cocoa
    powder, sifted
50 g (2 oz) hazelnuts,
    chopped

Cream the butter or margarine and sugar together until light and fluffy. Stir in the flour, cocoa and hazelnuts and mix well. Place teaspoonfuls of the mixture well apart on greased baking sheets (see note) and flatten with a dampened fork.

Bake in a preheated moderately hot oven, 200°C (400°F), Gas Mark 6, for 6 to 8 minutes, until pale golden.

Leave on the baking sheets for 1 minute then remove with a palette knife and place on a rolling pin to curl. Leave until set then remove very carefully.
Makes 20 to 24
NOTE: Do not bake more than 4 at a time or they will set before you have time to shape them.

CHOC-NUT TRUFFLES

250 g (8 oz) cake crumbs
125 g (4 oz) digestive
  biscuits, crushed
3 tablespoons cocoa
  powder
50 g (2 oz) hazelnuts,
  ground and browned
4 tablespoons apricot jam
4 tablespoons chocolate
  vermicelli

Mix the cake and biscuit crumbs, cocoa and hazelnuts together in a bowl. Add the jam and mix to a stiff paste.

Form the mixture into balls the size of a walnut and roll in the chocolate vermicelli.

Serve the truffles in paper cake cases.
Makes 16 to 18

CAKES AND GÂTEAUX

MOCHA GÂTEAU

3 eggs
125 g (4 oz) caster sugar
75 g (3 oz) plain flour,
  sifted
1 tablespoon instant coffee
  powder
TO FINISH:
250 g (8 oz) chocolate
  Crème au Beurre (see
  page 81)
50 g (2 oz) chocolate
  caraque (see page 10)
sifted icing sugar

Whisk the eggs and sugar together with an electric beater until thick and mousse-like. Fold in the flour and coffee powder. Pour into a lined and greased 20 cm (8 inch) cake tin and bake in a preheated moderately hot oven, 190°C (375°F), Gas Mark 5, for 35 to 40 minutes, until the cake springs back when pressed in the centre. Turn onto a wire rack to cool.

Split the cake in half, sandwich together with some of the crème au beurre and put on a plate. Use the remaining icing to cover the top and side of the cake.

Lay the chocolate caraque on top of the cake. Sprinkle with icing sugar.
Makes one 20 cm (8 inch) gâteau

CHOCOLATE LOG

SWISS ROLL:
3 size 1 eggs
125 g (4 oz) caster sugar
50 g (2 oz) plain flour
25 g (1 oz) cocoa powder
1 tablespoon hot water
TO FINISH:
125 g (4 oz) vanilla
  Butter Icing (see page 82)
250 g (8 oz) chocolate
  Butter Icing (see page 82)
sifted icing sugar

Make the Swiss roll as for Chocolate Swiss Roll (page 66). Unroll and remove the paper, spread with all but 2 tablespoons of the vanilla butter icing and roll up again carefully.

Cut a short diagonal wedge off one end of the roll and join it to the side with icing to resemble a branch. Place on a cake board.

Cover the log with the chocolate butter icing and mark lines to resemble the bark of a tree.

Place the remaining vanilla butter icing in a piping bag fitted with a No. 2 writing nozzle and pipe concentric circles of icing at each end of the log and the branch.

Sprinkle with icing sugar to look like snow and decorate with holly and berries.
Makes one chocolate log

CHOCOLATE AND CHERRY RING

250 g (8 oz) plain
    chocolate, broken into
    pieces
2 tablespoons clear honey
4 tablespoons milk
1 egg
125 g (4 oz) glacé
    cherries, quartered
400 g (14 oz) digestive
    biscuits, crushed
TOPPING:
50 g (2 oz) plain
    chocolate cake covering
1 tablespoon water
4 glacé cherries, halved

Place the chocolate, honey and milk in a large pan and heat gently until melted. Stir in the egg, cherries and biscuit crumbs and mix thoroughly. Turn into a greased 18 cm (7 inch) ring mould and press down firmly with a dampened palette knife. Chill in the refrigerator for 4 hours.

For the topping, heat the cake covering and water together, stirring occasionally, over gentle heat until melted. Dip the ring in hot water for a few seconds, then invert the cake onto a plate. Pour the topping over and decorate with the cherries.

Makes one 18 cm (7 inch) cake

CHOCOLATE SWISS ROLL

3 eggs
125 g (4 oz) caster sugar
50 g (2 oz) plain flour
25 g (1 oz) cocoa powder
1 tablespoon hot water
TO FINISH:
175 g (6 oz) vanilla
    Crème au Beurre (see
    page 81)
caster sugar to sprinkle

Whisk the eggs and sugar together with an electric beater until thick and mousse-like. Sift the flour with the cocoa and carefully fold in with a metal spoon, then fold in the water.

Turn into a lined and greased 20 × 30 cm (8 × 12 inch) Swiss roll tin and bake in a preheated moderately hot oven, 200°C (400°F), Gas Mark 6, for 8 to 10 minutes, until the cake springs back when lightly pressed.

Wring out a clean tea-towel in hot water. Lay it on a work surface, place a sheet of greaseproof paper on top and sprinkle lightly with caster sugar. Turn the sponge upside down onto the paper. Peel off the lining paper and trim edges. Cut two-thirds of the way through the short edge nearest you, then roll up with the paper inside. Hold in position for a few seconds, then place on a wire rack with the join underneath and leave to cool.

Unroll the cake and remove the paper. Spread the crème au beurre over the sponge and roll up again carefully. Sprinkle with sugar.

Makes one Swiss roll

WALNUT AND CHOCOLATE GÂTEAU

4 eggs
175 g (6 oz) caster sugar
75 g (3 oz) plain flour,
    sifted
125 g (4 oz) walnuts,
    ground
TO FINISH:
350 g (12 oz) vanilla
    Butter Icing (see page
    82)
2 tablespoons cocoa
    powder
2 tablespoons boiling
    water
50 g (2 oz) chopped
    walnuts
4 after dinner chocolate
    wafers, cut into
    triangles

Put the eggs and sugar in a bowl and whisk over a pan of hot water until thick and mousse-like. (The hot water is unnecessary if using an electric beater.) Partially fold in the flour, then add the nuts and fold in carefully.

Turn the mixture into a lined and greased deep 20 cm (8 inch) cake tin. Bake in a preheated moderately hot oven, 190°C (375°F), Gas Mark 5, for 30 to 35 minutes, until the cake springs back when lightly pressed. Turn onto a wire rack to cool.

Split the cake into three layers and sandwich them together with one third of the icing. Blend the cocoa with the water, cool, then beat into the remaining icing. Spread a little over the side of the cake and roll in the chopped walnuts to coat. Spread more icing on top of the cake and mark into swirls with a palette knife.

Spoon the remaining icing into a piping bag fitted with a fluted nozzle and pipe around the edge of the cake. Decorate with the chocolate wafers.
Makes one 20 cm (8 inch) gâteau

RICH CHOCOLATE CAKE

150 g (5 oz) plain
chocolate, chopped
4 tablespoons water
150 g (5 oz) butter or
margarine
150 g (5 oz) caster sugar
4 eggs, separated
125 g (4 oz) ground
almonds
50 g (2 oz) plain flour,
sifted
ICING:
175 g (6 oz) plain
chocolate, broken into
pieces
2 tablespoons milk
TO DECORATE:
10 walnut halves

Place the chocolate and water in a small pan and heat gently until melted, then cool slightly.

Cream the butter or margarine and sugar together until light and fluffy, then beat in the chocolate. Beat in the egg yolks then mix in the almonds and flour.

Whisk the egg whites until stiff, then fold into the cake mixture. Turn into a lined and greased 20 cm (8 inch) cake tin and bake in a preheated moderate oven, 160°C (325°F), Gas Mark 3, for 1 hour, or until firm in the centre. Leave in the tin for a few minutes, then cool on a wire rack.

To make the icing, place the chocolate and milk in a small pan and heat gently until melted, stirring occasionally; do *not* boil. Cool slightly, pour over the cake and spread evenly to coat completely.

Arrange the walnut halves around the top of the cake and leave until the icing is set.

Makes one 20 cm (8 inch) cake

CHOCOLATE FUDGE CAKE

125 g (4 oz) plain
  chocolate, chopped
300 ml (1/2 pint) milk
125 g (4 oz) butter or
  margarine
125 g (4 oz) soft brown
  sugar
2 eggs, separated
250 g (8 oz) self-raising
  flour
1/2 teaspoon baking
  powder
TO FINISH:
250 g (8 oz) Chocolate
  Fudge Icing (see page
  82), cooled and beaten
12-14 hazelnuts, browned

Place the chocolate and 4 tablespoons of the milk in a pan and heat gently, stirring, until melted. Stir in the remaining milk.

Cream the fat and sugar together until fluffy, then beat in the egg yolks one at a time. Sift flour and baking powder together. Add to the creamed mixture with three quarters of the chocolate milk; beat until smooth. Stir in remaining chocolate milk.

Whisk the egg whites until fairly stiff, then fold 1 tablespoon into the chocolate mixture to lighten it. Carefully fold in the rest.

Turn into 2 lined and greased 20 cm (8 inch) sandwich tins and bake in a preheated moderate oven, 180°C (350°F), Gas Mark 4, for 40 minutes, or until the cakes spring back when lightly pressed. Cool on a wire rack.

Use one third of the icing to sandwich the cakes together. Reheat the remaining icing gently to thin it slightly, then pour over the cake to coat completely. Arrange the nuts around the edge before the icing sets.
Makes one 20 cm (8 inch) cake

CHOCOLATE WHISKED SPONGE

50 g (2 oz) plain flour
25 g (1 oz) cocoa powder
3 eggs
125 g (4 oz) caster sugar
TO FINISH:
142 ml (5 fl oz) whipping
  cream, whipped
sifted icing sugar

Sift the flour and cocoa together. Put the eggs and sugar in a heatproof bowl over a pan of boiling water and whisk until the mixture is thick and mousse-like. (The hot water is unnecessary if using an electric beater.)

Fold in the flour mixture carefully. Turn into a lined and greased 20 cm (8 inch) cake tin. Bake in a preheated moderately hot oven, 190°C (375°F), Gas Mark 5, for 30 to 35 minutes, until the cake springs back when lightly pressed. Cool on a wire rack.

Split the cake in half and sandwich together with the cream. Sprinkle the top with icing sugar.
Makes one 20 cm (8 inch) cake

CHOCOLATE BANANA CAKE

*150 g (5 oz) self-raising
    flour*
*2 tablespoons cocoa
    powder*
*125 g (4 oz) butter or
    margarine*
*125 g (4 oz) soft brown
    sugar*
2 eggs
2 bananas, mashed
BANANA CREAM:
175 g (6 oz) cream cheese
2 small bananas, mashed
*1 tablespoon icing sugar,
    sifted*
TO FINISH:
*1 chocolate flake,
    crumbled*

Sift the flour and cocoa together and
set aside.

Cream the butter or margarine and
sugar together until fluffy. Add the
eggs one at time, adding a tablespoon
of the flour mixture with the second
egg. Fold in the remaining flour
mixture and the bananas.

Divide the mixture between 2 lined
and greased 18 cm (7 inch) sandwich
tins. Bake in a preheated moderate
oven, 180°C (350°F), Gas Mark 4, for
20 to 25 minutes, until the cakes
spring back when lightly pressed.
Turn onto a wire rack to cool.

To make the banana cream, beat
the cream cheese until smooth, then
mix in the banana and icing sugar.
Sandwich the cakes together with half
of the mixture; spread the remainder
over the top. Sprinkle the chocolate
flake around the edge of the cake.
Makes one 18 cm (7 inch) cake

CHOCOLATE ORANGE CAKE

*200 g (7 oz) self-raising
   flour*
*1/2 teaspoon baking
   powder*
*3 tablespoons cocoa
   powder*
*125 g (4 oz) soft brown
   sugar*
2 eggs
150 ml (1/4 pint) water
150 ml (1/4 pint) corn oil
TO FINISH:
*250 g (8 oz) orange
   Butter Icing (see page
   82)*
*50 g (2 oz) chocolate
   sugar strands*
*chocolate beanies or
   smarties*

Sift the dry ingredients into a mixing
bowl and make a well in the centre.
Add the eggs, water and oil and beat
thoroughly until smooth.

   Pour into 2 lined and greased 18 cm
(7 inch) sandwich tins and bake in a
preheated moderate oven, 160°C
(325°F), Gas Mark 3, for 25 to 30
minutes, until the cakes feel firm in
the centre. Leave in the tins for a few
minutes; turn onto a wire rack to cool.

   Sandwich the cakes together with a
quarter of the icing. Spread more
icing round the side and roll the cake
in the chocolate strands to coat. Cover
the top of the cake with icing and
mark into swirls with a palette knife.

   Put the remaining icing in a piping
bag fitted with a large fluted nozzle
and pipe rosettes around the top of
the cake. Decorate with the chocolate
beanies or smarties.
Makes one 18 cm (7 inch) cake

DEVIL'S FOOD CAKE

50 g (2 oz) cocoa powder
200 ml (⅓ pint) boiling
water
175 g (6 oz) plain flour
¼ teaspoon baking
powder
1 teaspoon bicarbonate of
soda
125 g (4 oz) butter or
margarine
300 g (10 oz) caster sugar
2 eggs, beaten
175 (6 oz) Chocolate
Butter Icing (see page
82)

QUICK AMERICAN
FROSTING:
175 g (6 oz) caster sugar
1 egg white
2 tablespoons hot water
pinch of cream of tartar

Blend the cocoa with half the water until smooth. Stir in the remaining water and leave to cool. Sift the flour, baking powder and soda together.

Cream the butter or margarine, sugar and 3 tablespoons of the blended cocoa together until light and fluffy. Gradually beat in the eggs.

Fold in the flour alternately with the remaining cocoa; the mixture may curdle but will not affect the result.

Divide the mixture between 2 lined and greased 20 cm (8 inch) sandwich tins and bake in a preheated moderate oven, 180°C (350°F), Gas Mark 4, for 45 to 50 minutes, until firm to the touch. Leave in the tins for 5 minutes, then turn onto a wire rack to cool.

Sandwich the cakes together with the butter icing. To make frosting, place all the ingredients in a bowl over a pan of hot water and whisk for 5 to 7 minutes until thick. Use immediately, swirling it on the top and side of the cake with a palette knife.
Makes one 20 cm (8 inch) cake

CHOCOLATE AND HAZELNUT SLICE

275 g (9 oz) plain
chocolate, broken into
pieces
1 × 170 g (6 oz) can
evaporated milk
300 g (10 oz) digestive
biscuits, crushed
125 g (4 oz) hazelnuts,
browned and ground

TO FINISH:
25 g (1 oz) plain
chocolate, melted

Place the chocolate in a pan with the milk and heat gently until melted.

Place the biscuit crumbs and hazelnuts in a bowl, pour on the melted chocolate and mix thoroughly.

Transfer to a lined and greased 500 g (1 lb) loaf tin and smooth the top with a palette knife. Leave in the refrigerator overnight.

Turn the cake out onto a serving plate. Spread three quarters of the chocolate over the top and leave to set. Place the remaining chocolate in a small greaseproof piping bag and drizzle over the top of the cake in lines. Cut into slices to serve.
Makes 15 slices

SACHERTORTE

175 g (6 oz) plain
 chocolate, broken into
 pieces
4 tablespoons milk
125 g (4 oz) butter or
 margarine
150 g (5 oz) caster sugar
5 eggs, separated
150 g (5 oz) plain flour,
 sifted

TO FINISH:
3 tablespoons apricot jam
175 g (6 oz) plain
 chocolate, broken into
 pieces
2 tablespoons single cream

Place the chocolate and milk in a small pan and heat gently until melted. Cool slightly.

Cream the butter or margarine and 75 g (3 oz) of the sugar together until light and fluffy, then beat in the egg yolks. Beat in the chocolate, then stir in the flour.

Whisk the egg whites until stiff, then whisk in the remaining sugar. Carefully fold into the cake mixture.

Turn into a lined and greased 20 cm (8 inch) cake tin and bake in a pre-heated moderate oven, 160°C (325°F), Gas Mark 3, for 1¼ to 1½ hours. Leave in tin for 5 minutes, then turn out carefully onto a wire rack to cool.

Split the cake in half and sandwich together with the jam.

Place the chocolate and cream in a small pan and heat gently, stirring, until smooth. Spread most of the chocolate over the top and side of the cake and leave to set. Place the remaining chocolate in a piping bag fitted with a writing nozzle and write 'Sacher' across the top.
Makes one 20 cm (8 inch) cake

CHOCOLATE CHESTNUT LAYER

Chocolate Whisked
  Sponge mixture (see
  page 70)
1 × 227 g (8 oz) can
  unsweetened chestnut
  purée
1 tablespoon clear honey
175 ml (6 fl oz) double
  cream
2 tablespoons Cointreau
125 g (4 oz) chocolate
  curls (see page 10)
8 chocolate rose leaves (see
  page 11)

Turn the whisked sponge mixture into a lined and greased 20 × 30 cm (8 × 12 inch) Swiss roll tin. Bake in a preheated moderately hot oven, 190°C (375°F), Gas Mark 5, for 20 to 25 minutes. Turn onto a wire rack to cool.

Place the chestnut purée, honey and 2 tablespoons of the cream in a bowl and beat thoroughly until smooth. Spoon half the mixture into a piping bag fitted with a 5 mm (¼ inch) fluted nozzle and set aside.

Whip the remaining cream until stiff, then whisk in the remaining chestnut purée and the Cointreau.

Cut the cake into 3 equal pieces and sandwich together with one third of the cream mixture. Cover the sides with more cream and coat with the chocolate curls. Spread remaining cream mixture over the top of the cake and mark with a palette knife.

Pipe the reserved chestnut purée around the edge of the cake and decorate with chocolate rose leaves.
Makes one 20 cm (8 inch) gâteau

CHOCOLATE VICTORIA SANDWICH

3 tablespoons cocoa
   powder
3 tablespoons boiling
   water
125 g (4 oz) butter or
   margarine
125 g (4 oz) caster sugar
2 eggs
125 g (4 oz) self-raising
   flour, sifted
TO FINISH:
175 g (6 oz) coffee Butter
   Icing (see page 82)
50 g (2 oz) chopped
   walnuts

Mix the cocoa with the water and
leave to cool.

Cream the butter or margarine and
sugar together until light and fluffy,
then beat in the blended cocoa.

Beat in the eggs one at a time,
adding a tablespoon of the flour with
the second egg. Fold in the remaining
flour carefully.

Divide the mixture between 2 lined
and greased 18 cm (7 inch) sandwich
tins and bake in a preheated moderate
oven, 180°C (350°F), Gas Mark 4, for
20 to 25 minutes, until the cakes
spring back when lightly pressed.
Turn onto a wire rack to cool.

Mix half the butter icing with half
the walnuts and use to sandwich the
cakes together. Spread the remaining
icing over the top of the cake and
mark into lines with a palette knife.
Sprinkle the remaining nuts in a
border around the edge of the cake.
Makes one 18 cm (7 inch) cake

MARBLED RING CAKE

2 tablespoons cocoa
 powder
2 tablespoons boiling
 water
175 g (6 oz) butter or
 margarine
175 g (6 oz) soft brown
 sugar
3 eggs, beaten
150 g (5 oz) self-raising
 flour, sifted
TO FINISH:
250 g (8 oz) coffee
 Fudge Icing (see page
 82)
25 g (1 oz) plain
 chocolate, melted

Mix the cocoa with the boiling water to form a smooth paste and set aside.

Cream butter or margarine and sugar together until light and fluffy. Beat in the eggs one at a time, adding a tablespoon of flour with the last two. Carefully fold in the remaining flour.

Place half the mixture in a separate bowl and mix in the cocoa paste. Spoon the mixtures alternately into a greased and floured 23 cm (9 inch) ring mould. Bake in a preheated moderate oven, 180°C (350°F), Gas Mark 4, for 40 minutes, until the cake springs back when lightly pressed. Turn onto a wire rack to cool.

Pour over the coffee fudge icing, spread with a palette knife to cover completely, and leave to set.

Put the warm chocolate in a greaseproof paper piping bag, snip off the tip and drizzle the chocolate across the cake in lines.
Makes one 23 cm (9 inch) cake

ICINGS AND SAUCES

CRÈME GANACHE

175 g (6 oz) plain
   chocolate, broken into
   pieces
4 tablespoons single cream
50 g (2 oz) butter, cut
   into cubes
2 egg yolks
1 tablespoon rum

Place the chocolate in a small pan with the cream and heat gently until melted. Cool slightly, then beat in the butter a little at a time. Beat in the egg yolks and rum and leave until cool and firm, stirring occasionally.

This quantity is sufficient to fill and cover a 20 cm (8 inch) sandwich cake.

Makes a 250 g (8 oz) mixture

NOTE: Crème Ganache can also be used as a thin, coating icing. Pour it over the cake while it is still warm.

If the icing is to be used for piping (as below) allow it to become quite cold and firm. Beat thoroughly before using.

CRÈME AU BEURRE

2 egg whites
125 g (4 oz) icing sugar,
  sifted
125 g (4 oz) unsalted
  butter
½ teaspoon vanilla
  essence

Whisk the egg whites until very stiff, then gradually whisk in the icing sugar until thick.

Cream the butter until very soft, then beat in the meringue mixture a little at a time with the vanilla essence. If the mixture curdles, warm the bowl and continue whisking.

This quantity is sufficient to fill and ice the top of a 20 cm (8 inch) sandwich cake.

Makes a 125 g (4 oz) mixture

Chocolate Crème au Beurre: Add 75 g (3 oz) plain chocolate, melted and cooled, with the meringue mixture and beat thoroughly.

CHOCOLATE FUDGE ICING

50 g (2 oz) butter or
    margarine
3 tablespoons milk
250 g (8 oz) icing sugar,
    sifted
2 tablespoons cocoa
    powder, sifted

Place the butter or margarine and milk in a small pan and heat gently until melted. Add the icing sugar and cocoa and beat until smooth and glossy. Cool slightly, then pour over the cake, spreading with a palette knife to cover completely.

This quantity is sufficient to cover a 20 cm (8 inch) sandwich cake.

Makes a 250 g (8 oz) mixture

NOTE: This icing can also be used as a filling if allowed to cool completely; beat during cooling to prevent a skin forming.

Coffee Fudge Icing: Replace the cocoa with instant coffee powder.

BUTTER ICING

75 g (3 oz) butter or
    margarine
250 g (8 oz) icing sugar,
    sifted
2 tablespoons milk
½ teaspoon vanilla
    essence

Beat the butter or margarine with half the icing sugar until smooth and creamy. Add the remaining icing sugar with the milk and vanilla essence and beat thoroughly until smooth.

This quantity is sufficient to fill and cover a 20 cm (8 inch) sandwich cake.

Makes a 250 g (8 oz) mixture

Orange or Lemon Butter Icing:
Add the grated rind of 1 orange or lemon when beating the butter or margarine and sugar. Replace the milk with orange or lemon juice.

Chocolate Butter Icing: Blend 2 tablespoons cocoa powder with 2 tablespoons boiling water. Cool, then add to the creamed mixture with only 1 tablespoon milk.

Coffee Butter Icing: Replace 1 tablespoon milk with 1 tablespoon coffee essence.

BITTER CHOCOLATE SAUCE

175 g (6 oz) plain chocolate, broken into pieces
150 ml (¼ pint) water
1 teaspoon instant coffee powder
50 g (2 oz) sugar

Place all the ingredients in a small pan and heat gently until the sugar has dissolved. Bring to the boil and simmer gently for 10 minutes. Serve hot or cold, with ice cream, sponge puddings, pears and profiteroles.
Makes 300 ml (½ pint)

CHOCOLATE ORANGE SAUCE

125 g (4 oz) plain chocolate, broken into pieces
juice of 1 orange
1 × 170 g (6 oz) can evaporated milk
2 tablespoons Cointreau

Place all the ingredients, except the Cointreau, in a small pan and heat gently until melted. Bring to the boil and simmer for 3 minutes, then add the Cointreau. Serve warm or cold, with ices and chocolate sponge.
Makes 450 ml (¾ pint)

FUDGE SAUCE

1 × 170 g (6 oz) can
  evaporated milk
50 g (2 oz) plain
  chocolate, broken into
  pieces
50 g (2 oz) soft dark
  brown sugar

Place all the ingredients in a pan; heat gently until the sugar has dissolved. Bring to the boil and simmer for 3 minutes. Serve warm or cold.
Makes 250 ml (8 fl oz)

Coffee Fudge Sauce: Replace chocolate with 1 teaspoon each instant coffee powder and cornflour.

MINT-CHOC SAUCE

175 g (6 oz) plain
  chocolate, in pieces
284 ml (10 fl oz) single
  cream
50 g (2 oz) caster sugar
1 teaspoon peppermint
  essence

Place the chocolate, cream and sugar in a small pan and heat gently until the sugar has dissolved. Bring to the boil and simmer for 2 minutes, then stir in the peppermint essence. Serve hot or cold, with ice cream.
Makes 450 ml (¾ pint)

SWEETS AND DRINKS

CHOCOLATE CHERRIES

50 g (2 oz) ground almonds
50 g (2 oz) icing sugar, sifted
1 egg yolk
1 teaspoon lemon juice
few drops almond essence
16 glacé cherries
125 g (4 oz) plain chocolate, melted
25 g (1 oz) milk chocolate, melted

Place the almonds, icing sugar, egg yolk, lemon juice and almond essence in a bowl and mix together to form a paste. Divide into 16 pieces and mould one piece around each cherry to form a ball.

Using a skewer, dip each cherry ball into the plain chocolate; place on a baking sheet lined with greaseproof paper and leave until set. Pipe a design on top with the cooled milk chocolate. Serve in paper sweet cases.

Makes 16

COLETTES

20 split almonds, browned
125 g (4 oz) plain
   chocolate, melted
175 g (6 oz) Crème
   Ganache (see page 80)

Dip half of each almond in the melted chocolate and leave on greaseproof paper to dry.

Spoon a little melted chocolate into 20 paper sweet cases and, using the handle of a teaspoon, spread it all over the inside. Leave to set, then cover with a second coat of chocolate; leave to set.

Carefully remove the paper case. Spoon the crème ganache into a piping bag fitted with a large fluted nozzle and pipe a whirl into each chocolate case. Top with the almonds.

Makes 20

MAGIC MINTIES

25 g (1 oz) butter or
    margarine
150 g (5 oz) plain
    chocolate, broken into
    pieces
2 tablespoons water
125 g (4 oz) digestive
    biscuits, crushed
½ teaspoon peppermint
    essence
TO FINISH (optional):
75 g (3 oz) plain
    chocolate, melted

Place the butter or margarine, chocolate and water in a pan and heat gently until melted. Stir in the biscuit crumbs and peppermint essence and mix thoroughly. Allow to cool.

Turn onto a strip of foil. Shape into a roll about 3.5 cm (1½ inches) in diameter, wrapping the roll in the foil, then form into a cylindrical shape. Cut into 5 mm (¼ inch) slices. Partially coat with the chocolate as for Praline Diamonds (opposite) if desired.

Makes 20

PRALINE DIAMONDS

PRALINE:
75 g (3 oz) caster sugar
75 g (3 oz) whole
  unblanched almonds
MOCHA:
250 g (8 oz) plain
  chocolate, broken into
  pieces
3 tablespoons black coffee
TO FINISH *(optional)*:
125 g (4 oz) plain
  chocolate, melted

To make the praline, place the sugar and almonds in a small heavy-based pan and heat very gently until the sugar caramelizes and the almonds begin to split. Turn onto an oiled baking sheet and leave until cool, then crush in a mouli-grater or in a food processor.

Place the chocolate and coffee in a pan and heat very gently until melted. Stir in the praline mixture and turn into a lined and greased shallow 15 cm (6 inch) square tin. Leave to set, then turn out and cut into diamond shapes.

Dip one end of each diamond into the melted chocolate, if using. Allow the excess to drip away, then place on a baking sheet lined with greaseproof paper to set.

Serve in paper sweet cases.
Makes 24

CHOCOLATE RUM TRUFFLES

175 g (6 oz) plain
  chocolate, broken into
  pieces
2 tablespoons single cream
  or top of the milk
1 egg yolk
1 tablespoon rum
1 tablespoon cocoa powder

Place the chocolate and cream or milk in a small pan and heat gently until melted. Add the egg yolk and rum and mix thoroughly. Leave in a cool place to chill until firm enough to handle.

Roll teaspoonfuls of the mixture into small balls. Place the cocoa in a small plastic bag, drop in a few truffles at a time and shake until coated. Serve in paper sweet cases.
Makes about 20

Orange Truffles: Replace the rum with orange juice and add the grated rind of 1 orange. Shake in chocolate vermicelli instead of cocoa.

Mocha Truffles: Dissolve 2 teaspoons instant coffee in 1 tablespoon boiling water and use instead of the rum. Shake in finely chopped walnuts or almonds instead of cocoa.

HAZELNUT CLUSTERS

*250 g (8 oz) plain
  chocolate, broken into
  pieces*
*25 g (1 oz) butter or
  margarine*
*150 g (5 oz) hazelnuts,
  browned*
125 g (4 oz) raisins

Place the chocolate and butter or
margarine in a heatproof bowl over a
pan of hot water and heat gently until
melted. Stir in the nuts and raisins.

Place teaspoonfuls of the mixture
on a baking sheet lined with
greaseproof paper and leave to set.
Serve in paper sweet cases.
Makes 26 to 30

CHOCOLATE STRAWBERRIES

*250 g (8 oz) firm
  strawberries, with hulls*
*125 g (4 oz) plain
  chocolate, melted*

Hold each strawberry by the stem
and dip the end into the chocolate.
Allow the excess chocolate to drip
off, then place on a baking sheet lined
with greaseproof paper to set.
Makes 15 to 20

CHOCOLATE FUDGE

125 g (4 oz) butter or margarine
4 tablespoons water
2 tablespoons cocoa powder
2 tablespoons golden syrup
625 g (1¼ lb) caster sugar
175 ml (6 fl oz) condensed milk

Place the butter or margarine, water, cocoa and syrup in a large heavy-based pan and heat gently until melted. Add the sugar and heat very gently until dissolved; this may take 30 minutes, but it must be done gently, *without boiling*.

Add the condensed milk and bring to the boil, stirring. Boil for 5 to 10 minutes, until the bubbles look like 'erupting volcanoes' and a spoonful forms a soft ball when dropped into a glass of cold water.

Cool until the bubbling stops, then beat well for about 5 minutes, until the mixture begins to thicken; this will give a smooth texture. Turn into a greased 18 × 28 cm (7 × 11 inch) Swiss roll tin and leave for about 30 minutes, until half set. Mark into 2.5 cm (1 inch) squares with a sharp knife and leave until cold. Cut into squares, remove from the tin and store in a jar.
Makes about 750 g (1½ lb)

HOT CHOCOLATE FROTH

25 g (1 oz) plain
  chocolate
300 ml (½ pint) boiling
  milk
½ teaspoon coffee
  granules

Place the chocolate and boiling milk
in an electric blender or food
processor and blend on maximum
speed for 15 seconds. Pour into mugs
and sprinkle with coffee granules to
serve.
Serves 2

CHOCOLATE MILK SHAKE

300 ml (½ pint) milk
1 tablespoon drinking
  chocolate
2 scoops vanilla ice cream
chocolate curls (see page
  11) to decorate

Place all the ingredients, except
1 scoop ice cream, in an electric blender
or food processor and blend on
maximum speed for 15 seconds. Pour
into tumblers and top with remaining
ice cream. Serve immediately,
sprinkled with chocolate curls.
Serves 2

Vanilla Milk Shake: Replace the
drinking chocolate with 2 teaspoons
caster sugar.

CHOCOLATE MINT COOLER

25 g (1 oz) plain
  chocolate, chopped
2 tablespoons hot water
¼ teaspoon peppermint
  essence
300 ml (½ pint) milk
2 scoops vanilla ice cream
grated chocolate to
  decorate

Place the chocolate and hot water in an electric blender or food processor and blend on maximum speed for 10 seconds. Add the remaining ingredients and blend for 15 seconds. Pour into tall glasses and sprinkle with grated chocolate to serve.
Serves 2

ICED CHOCOLATE MILK

25 g (1 oz) plain
  chocolate, chopped
4 tablespoons boiling
  water
300 ml (½ pint) milk
2 tablespoons whipped
  cream

Place the chocolate and boiling water in an electric blender or food processor and blend on maximum speed for 10 seconds. Add the milk and blend for a further 10 seconds. Allow to cool, then chill before serving, topped with a whirl of whipped cream.
Serves 2

INDEX

ACKNOWLEDGMENTS
Photography by Paul Williams
Food prepared by Carole Handslip
Photographic stylist: Penny Markham